Safari
PATTERNS

by Elizabeth Bennett

SCHOLASTIC INC.

**Leopards
have lots of**

SMALL
SPOTS.

They can climb trees
to look out for
prey below.

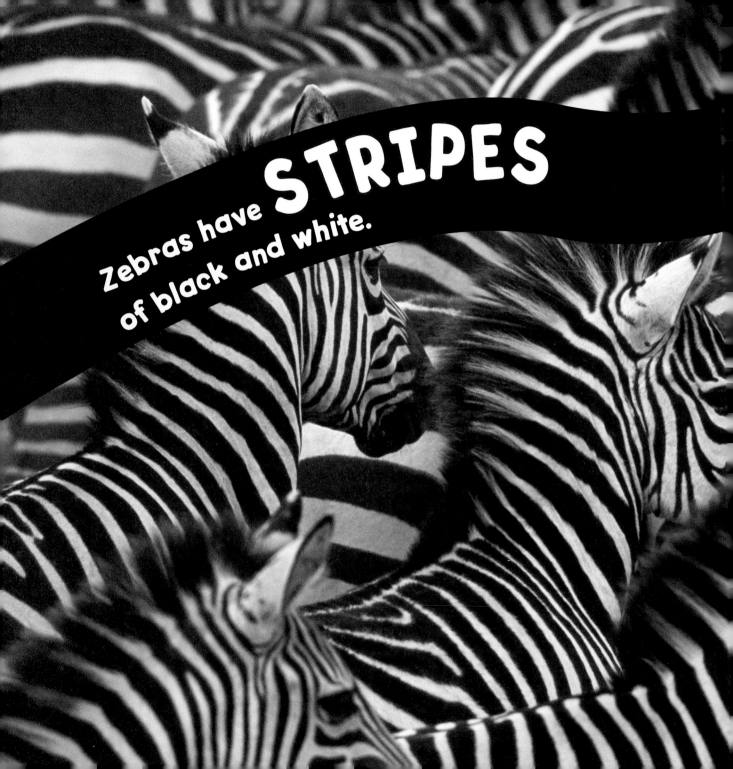

Zebras have **STRIPES** of black and white.

But no two zebras have exactly the same stripes.

Bongos have
STRIPES,
too!

They usually have a different number of stripes on each side.

Even leaves have

STRIPES.

This banana
leaf can grow
to be as big
as a car!

This elephant's

WRINKLY

skin forms a pattern.

The wrinkles help keep
the elephant cool in
the African heat.

These leaves make a beautiful **PATTERN.**

The thick leaves collect water for the plant.

TAKE A CLOSER LOOK!

PATTERNS

Bongos, which live in the tropical jungles of central Africa, usually have a different number of stripes on each side.

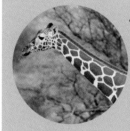
The brown-and-white pattern on a **giraffe** helps it blend in with the light and shade of the savanna woodlands.

The leaves on a **banana tree** are waterproof and can be used as plates for serving food.

Leopards are sometimes confused with two other large spotted cats: the cheetah, which also lives in Africa, and the jaguar, which lives in Central and South America.

The wrinkles on an **elephant's skin** help it to stay cool. African elephants have more wrinkles than Asian elephants because Asian elephants live in cooler jungles.

When a **zebra** stands in a big group, its pattern of stripes blends in with zebras around it. It is hard for hungry lions to figure out which zebra to hunt, so they often give up.

The leaves on this **giant lobelia** plant help collect water. The water protects the plant from the extreme cold temperatures during the night in the Kenyan mountains.